INSIDE STEVEN COHEN'S EMPIRE

The Truth About Finance And Insider Trading

Prabal Jain

Riverwood Capital

Riverwood Capital

ISBN: 9798867980306

CONTENTS

INTRODUCTION

The Meteoric Rise of a Trading Mogul

In the realms of high finance, few names echo with as much resonance as that of Steven A. Cohen. Starting his journey as a small-time options trader, Cohen eventually vaulted into the annals of Wall Street as one of the most successful hedge fund managers ever witnessed. His venture, SAC Capital, not only etched his name in gold but also generated returns that became the envy of the financial world. Cohen's track record was nothing short of breathtaking, creating a clamor amongst investors who desperately wanted a slice of the success that seemed to follow him. Yet, every tale of triumph hosts shadows of intrigue, and Cohen's story is no different. His ability to churn out a staggering 60% return annually became a beacon for the federal eye, stirring the waters of a multiyear investigation into the rumored insider trading practices rampant amongst Wall Street hedge funds.

The Eye of the Storm

November 2010 marked a pivotal turn in this . As the ink dried on a Wall Street Journal article detailing a years-long government probe into insider trading within Wall Street's prestigious hedge funds, tremors of anxiety rippled across the financial district. This investigation had unveiled a trail leading from ordinary traders to information brokers, and eventually to the hallowed halls of SAC Capital. One of the names prominently featured was that of Donald Longueuil, a trader whose affiliations with SAC Capital painted a target on his back.

Panic Unveiled

As Longueuil skimmed through the article on a chilly Friday night in New York's Upper East Side, fear replaced the blood in his veins. It was clear that the government's crosshairs were aligning on him and his colleagues. In a desperate attempt to obliterate any incriminating evidence, Longueuil dismembered several of his computer hard drives that night. He meticulously recounted his actions in a recorded conversation with his colleague, Noah Freeman, detailing how he separated the remains into four little baggies and embarked on a 20-block walk around the city, scattering pieces of what once held secrets, now shards of a tale that was slowly unraveling.

CHAPTER 1: THE DOWNFALL BECKONS

The frantic actions of Donald Longueuil, as he dismantled hard drives to erase trails of incriminating evidence, showcased a tangible shift from covert operations to desperate measures. The conversations captured between Longueuil and Noah Freeman, both former SAC employees, painted a vivid image of panic. As they recounted the disposal of evidence in the dark alleys of the city, the harsh reality of their actions and the looming scrutiny started to take form. Their desperate acts were not enough to elude the clutches of the law; both Longueuil and Freeman were ensnared by the government's tightening noose, their guilty pleas resounding through the halls of SAC Capital.

The Spectre of Insider Trading

The arrest of two former portfolio managers of SAC Capital seemed to confirm the whispers that had long circulated through Wall Street. The allegations of insider trading within the prestigious walls of Stevie Cohen's empire were now headlines, casting a long, dark shadow over SAC Capital. The arrests may have been shocking to some, but for many in the trading circles, it was a scenario long anticipated. The casual discussions about insider trading at SAC Capital had transitioned from being Wall Street's open secret to a stark reality.

The Skepticism Runs Deep

The commonality of the jests regarding insider trading at SAC Capital underpinned a culture where ethical boundaries appeared to be a mere suggestion. The inquisitive probes were often met with hearty laughter, not out of ignorance, but from a place of deep-seated skepticism and acceptance of a murky moral compass. This perception was not just limited to the bystanders; it was a that found resonance even within the closed quarters of SAC Capital.

The Man Behind the Curtain

At the epicenter of these swirling storms stood Steven A. Cohen, the enigmatic founder and CEO of SAC Capital. Though he maintained a stoic silence in public regarding the allegations, his deposition in 2011 shed some light on his perspective. The video deposition, part of a civil lawsuit against SAC, was a rare glimpse into Cohen's understanding or lack thereof, of the regulations governing insider trading. His unfamiliarity with Rule 10b5-1, the Securities and Exchange Commission's cornerstone regulation against insider trading, was baffling. His assertion that the law surrounding insider trading was vague, underscored a concerning ambiguity in the ethical framework that guided the operations of SAC Capital.

The Formative Wilderness

Upon graduating from the prestigious Wharton Business School in the late 1970s, Steven Cohen set foot on the bustling streets of Wall Street, a world teeming with ambition and cut-throat competition. The financial world soon came to know of Cohen, not just as another trader, but as a legend in the making. His Midas touch in trading didn't just earn him a place among the elites; it catapulted him into a league of his own. The persona of Steve Cohen started symbolizing an unyielding drive to amass wealth, a quality revered by his contemporaries. He wasn't just making money; he was crafting one of the great American fortunes, predominantly on the back of his own trading prowess.

The Crucible: Gruntal & Co

The cornerstone of Cohen's illustrious career was laid at a relatively modest brokerage firm on Wall Street known as Gruntal & Co. Despite its middling reputation, Gruntal provided a fertile ground for Cohen to hone his trading skills. The environment was reminiscent of the Wild West, where the law of the land was to "eat what you kill." This ethos allowed traders to retain a significant chunk of their profits, a liberty that was scarce in the more established firms. It was within these less restrained corridors that Cohen fine-tuned his ability to "read the tape" and trade stocks, essentially laying the foundation of his trading acumen.

Learning the Ropes, For Better or Worse

Gruntal & Co. was more than just a trading floor; it was a crucible that molded Cohen's approach towards trading. The conversations on the street whispered that Gruntal was the kind of place where one could get a real education on insider trading, among other less-than-ethical practices. Indeed, the firm had its fair share of run-ins with regulators. It was a place where sanctions for insider trading weren't unheard of, and the management often found itself embroiled in various regulatory tangles.

Fast forward to the times of scrutiny, when Cohen's understanding of trading regulations, particularly regarding material nonpublic information, came under the spotlight, the veil of ambiguity seemed to shroud his responses. His claim of the laws being vague and open to interpretation could very well have been a reflection of the laissez-faire environment that incubated his trading career. The norms, or the lack thereof, at Gruntal might have contributed to a mindset that viewed regulatory boundaries as blurry lines rather than clear demarcations.

◆ ◆ ◆

CHAPTER 2: THE DAWN OF SAC CAPITAL

With a taste of success and a small fortune amassed at Gruntal, Steven Cohen yearned for grander arenas to exhibit his trading prowess. The year 1992 saw Cohen bid adieu to Gruntal, armed with a hefty bank balance and a vision to carve his own niche in the financial jungle. With a significant portion of his amassed wealth, Cohen inaugurated his venture, a hedge fund named SAC Capital. This wasn't just a new beginning for Cohen but the birth of a distinctive kind of hedge fund that would soon become a force to reckon with.

Redefining Hedge Funds

The concept of hedge funds wasn't new; they had been around since the 1940s. However, the 1990s brought with it a wave of disillusionment among traders towards the bureaucratic shackles of big investment banks. This dissonance propelled many to seek independence, leading to a surge in the establishment of hedge funds. These funds were initially conceived as financial cushions, providing a hedge against the volatile market swings, thereby offering a semblance of security to affluent investors.

As the curtains of the millennium drew near, the calm demeanor of hedge funds began to morph. Propelled by a few high-flying funds delivering astonishing returns, the perception of hedge funds transitioned from being mere safe havens to lucrative investment avenues. The whispers of extraordinary returns soon turned into roaring affirmations, setting new expectations among investors. The once sleepy domain of hedge funds was now a bustling marketplace, with investors flocking in hopes of amplifying their wealth.

SAC Capital: The Outlier

In the proliferating landscape of hedge funds, SAC Capital emerged as a notable outlier. While others were basking in the new found glory, Cohen's venture was scripting a success that was unparalleled. The returns generated by SAC Capital weren't just impressive; they were in a league of their own. The enigmatic aura surrounding Cohen thickened as his fund continued to defy market norms and expectations. The legend of Steven A. Cohen was not just thriving; it was leading the charge in a rapidly evolving financial arena.

The High Stakes of Information

Steven Cohen's SAC Capital was not just known for its extraordinary returns, but also for its audacious fee structure. While the industry standard rested at a "two and twenty" model—charging two percent of the assets under management and twenty percent of the profits—Cohen upped the ante significantly. SAC Capital's fee structure was a staggering "three and fifty," charging three percent of assets and a whopping fifty percent of any gains. This aggressive approach was not met with disdain but rather with a rush of investors wanting to get a piece of the action. The rationale was straightforward: Cohen's track record was nothing short of mesmerizing, and everyone wanted in.

In his initial seven-year run, Cohen's magic touch seemed almost invincible with just three losing months, the worst being a mere two percent decline. His knack for outperforming the market was largely rooted in his rapid trading strategy, particularly around the quarterly earnings announcements of companies. Whether a stock soared or plummeted post-earnings, Cohen had a way of positioning his trades to reap benefits. This tactic wasn't merely about trading stocks but mastering the art of trading information.

The Quest for the "Edge"

The cornerstone of Cohen's strategy lay in an incessant pursuit of an "edge"—a term frequently tossed around in hedge fund circles, implying a unique information advantage. It was about knowing something crucial before the rest of the market caught wind of it. Cohen's approach was emblematic of an information-driven hedge fund, thriving on every shred of intel that could provide a trading advantage. The name of the game was to gather as much information as possible to navigate the market currents adeptly.

This relentless hunt for an edge blurred the line between legal and illegal in the information game. This wasn't unique to SAC Capital. Turney Duff, a former employee at The Galleon Group, another hedge fund, shed light on the industry-wide obsession with information. Led by Raj Rajaratnam, The Galleon Group's ethos mirrored the industry's sentiment—it was all about information. Trading stocks was merely a facade; the real commodity was information.

The Currency of Connections

In the high-octane landscape of hedge funds, information is the elixir that fuels fortunes. Turney Duff's recounting of his days at The Galleon Group unveils the relentless pursuit of information that defined the hedge fund culture. It was less about trading stocks and more about trading information. The nights spent in New York's upscale restaurants and clubs were not mere social escapades, but strategic moves to cultivate relationships that could unlock valuable information.

Networking: The Unseen Asset

For traders like Duff and those at SAC Capital, networking

wasn't a choice but a necessity. Each contact, regardless of their professional backdrop, was a potential treasure trove of information. Whether it was a casual acquaintance who had insights into upcoming media coverage, or a friend whose father might have knowledge about a drug awaiting FDA approval, every relationship was a conduit to information that could catalyze lucrative trades.

Wall Street: The Nexus of Information

The symbiotic relationship between hedge funds and Wall Street firms epitomized the essence of information trading. Hedge funds, with their incessant market activity, were golden geese for brokers, generating hefty commissions. In return, Wall Street rolled out its best information to these funds, fostering a cycle that thrived on information exchange. The hierarchy of this relationship was clear—the more commissions a fund generated for a firm, the higher it climbed on the priority list for receiving crucial market information, a practice known as the "first call."

Steven Cohen was acutely aware of the power of the "first call" and was more than willing to pay the price for this privilege. Rumors abounded that Cohen's strategy included paying exorbitant commissions to secure a spot as a top-tier fee payer on Wall Street. This wasn't just about garnering favor; it was a calculated investment to ensure that when vital information flowed through the financial veins of Wall Street, SAC Capital was among the first to receive it.

The Empire and the Enigma

Over a span of two decades, SAC Capital burgeoned into a colossal entity in the hedge fund realm, with Steven Cohen at its helm amassing wealth that epitomized the American dream. His asset portfolio boasted a sprawling mansion in Greenwich, Connecticut, a luxurious beach house in the Hamptons, multiple lavish apartments in Manhattan, and an awe-inspiring modern art collection. Cohen's philanthropic endeavors reflected his financial stature, as he generously donated tens of millions to charitable causes. The persona of 'King Cohen', as illustrated in his 2002 Christmas cards, wasn't just a whimsical portrayal but a reflection of his financial dominion.

Cohen's ability to deliver staggering returns year after year left the financial world both in awe and skepticism. The math was simple yet astonishing. To provide a return of 50% to investors after taking his share of 50% of the profits meant he was essentially doubling the money. The consistency with which SAC Capital yielded around 30% returns to investors, post-expenses, was a financial marvel. This level of profitability catapulted Cohen's personal fortune to a staggering $8 billion by 2008.

CHAPTER 3: THE SHROUDED TRAIL OF INSIDER TRADING

The extraordinary returns emanating from SAC Capital soon became a siren song for federal scrutiny. The question on everyone's mind was clear: How was Cohen able to sustain such an astronomical rate of profitability? The veil of secrecy around Cohen's strategies and the murmurs of 'first calls' began to paint a picture of a financial empire that might have thrived on the edge of legality.

The Galleon Group: A Prelude to Inquiry

The government's investigative lens first focused on another hedge fund, The Galleon Group, led by CEO Raj Rajaratnam. The relaxed and clubby ambiance of The Galleon Group was a stark contrast to the enigmatic aura surrounding SAC Capital. Rajaratnam, with his charismatic and bubbly persona, led a successful yet free-wheeling hedge fund, which soon found itself under the federal scanner. The investigation that began with The Galleon Group soon meandered its way towards the towering gates of SAC Capital.

The relaxed ambiance at The Galleon Group concealed a more obscure aspect of its trading activities. Turney Duff's recollection of a peculiar phone call during Raj Rajaratnam's absence unveiled a glimpse of the clandestine information channels that thrived within the hedge fund. The whispered tip about an imminent upgrade for Amazon by Jefferies, a notable brokerage firm, pushed Duff into a moral and legal quandary. Despite the internal conflict, the allure of substantial profits prevailed as Duff purchased

100,000 shares of Amazon, reaping a windfall of half a million dollars within 30 seconds. This incident underscored the potent allure and the murky ethics surrounding insider information in the hedge fund industry.

Probing Sedna Capital

The transitions to 2006, when John Moon, a lawyer at UBS, stumbled upon suspicious trading activities at a hedge fund called Sedna Capital. The red flags were raised regarding violations concerning "friends and family" money. This term typically refers to investments made by close associates or relatives in a fund, and there are specific regulations governing such transactions to prevent conflicts of interest and unfair trading practices.

Moon's scrutiny of Sedna Capital opened a can of worms that hinted at deeper, systemic issues within the hedge fund industry. The peculiar trading patterns and the subsequent investigations were indicative of a larger that had been playing out behind the closed doors of many hedge funds. The probe into Sedna Capital's dealings was a prelude to a more expansive investigation that would soon entangle some of the most prominent figures in the hedge fund industry.

The saga involving Galleon, Sedna Capital, and the whispered tips underscored the precarious balance between aggressive trading strategies and the boundaries of legality. The relentless pursuit of an "edge" had spiraled into a murky realm where the lines between legal foresight and insider trading were dangerously blurred. The unfolding events were a harbinger of the storm that was brewing, threatening to shake the very foundations of the hedge fund industry.

The Two Faces of Sedna Capital

John Moon's probe into Sedna Capital unveiled a troubling scenario. The hedge fund seemed to have a dual structure: one for public investors and another for "friends and family." The allocation of trades appeared skewed, favoring the latter with profitable trades while saddling the public investors with losses. The timing of certain trades raised eyebrows, prompting Moon to escalate the matter to the Securities and Exchange Commission (SEC).

The intrigue deepened with the revelation that Sedna was run by Rengan Rajaratnam, brother to Galleon Group's CEO, Raj Rajaratnam. The SEC suspected an insider trading nexus between the brothers, triggering a request for Raj Rajaratnam's records. The findings led them to Roomy Khan, a Silicon Valley executive with a history of insider trading.

The Path to Roomy Khan

Khan's recent communications with Rajaratnam prompted the FBI to step in. Agent BJ Kang was dispatched to California to confront Khan, outlining the severity of her situation and offering a way out through cooperation. The stakes were laid bare: Khan was embroiled in a serious investigation that could alter her life dramatically.

Khan's decision to cooperate with the FBI marked a pivotal moment in the investigation. The FBI extended its dragnet, focusing on Rajaratnam's employees in New York. An extensive surveillance operation unfolded, shadowing potential informants from their homes to their workplaces, keenly observing their interactions. The meticulous groundwork laid by the investigators was the precursor to delving deeper into the clandestine world of insider trading that seemingly thrived within the echelons of Galleon Group and potentially beyond.

Informants: The Linchpin of Investigation

The cooperation of insiders like Roomy Khan was instrumental in piercing through the veil of secrecy that shrouded the illicit trading activities. As agents meticulously pieced together the puzzle, the silhouette of a vast network of information trading began to emerge, hinting at a pervasive culture of insider trading that had ensnared not just Galleon, but possibly other players in the Wall Street arena.

The Unraveling of Galleon's Tapestry

The FBI's focus shifted to David Slaine, a trader once associated with Galleon Group. Known for his intimidating demeanor, Slaine was a notable figure on Wall Street. In June 2007, the FBI orchestrated a discreet encounter with Slaine, leading to his cooperation with the authorities.

Cracking the Inner Circle

Slaine's collaboration proved to be a watershed moment. He unveiled a network of connections Raj Rajaratnam maintained with high-profile individuals from his alma mater, Wharton Business School. Many of these contacts had ascended to executive positions in large corporations, providing Rajaratnam with a plethora of insider information.

A Surfeit of Corrupt Funds

As agents Carroll and Chaves consolidated their findings, the extent of corruption within Wall Street's hedge fund circuit became apparent. A significant number of funds were engaged in a network of illicit information sharing, far surpassing initial estimations. The magnitude of the issue evoked a realization that the investigation had unveiled a gargantuan challenge.

Wiretaps: A Novel Tactic

In an unprecedented move, late 2007 saw the FBI securing authorization for wiretapping Galleon traders, including Raj Rajaratnam. This marked the first instance of employing wiretaps in an insider trading investigation, a tactic traditionally reserved for combating organized crime or terrorism. This novel approach signaled the gravity with which authorities were now treating white-collar crime.

The Unveiling of Conversational Riches

Wiretaps unearthed a trove of candid discussions among traders about their illicit activities, providing investigators with unfiltered insight into the clandestine operations of insider trading rings. The casual demeanor with which these individuals discussed their illegal trades was a testament to the ingrained culture of insider trading within these circles.

The Wiretap Chronicles

The usage of wiretaps, though highly effective, presented a unique set of challenges. The vast amount of conversations revolving around trading required meticulous scrutiny to distinguish between normal trading discussions and those hinting at insider trading. It was a tedious process with a high probability of overlooking critical pieces of information.

A particular call intercepted between Rajaratnam and another trader showcased the minutiae of their daily interactions, focused on positions and updates on companies like Synaptics. The exchange of such detailed information was routine, making the task of identifying illegal trades significantly difficult.

Rajaratnam's network of informants spanned various levels of corporate hierarchy and the financial sector. One particularly intriguing character was Danielle Chiesi, a hedge fund manager with a flamboyant persona. Her liaisons extended beyond professional boundaries, as exemplified by her romantic involvement with an IBM executive, which became a channel for acquiring insider information.

The Seductress of Insider Trading

Chiesi's affair with the IBM executive unveiled a gray zone where personal relationships intertwined with professional misconduct. This relationship was emblematic of the lengths individuals would go to obtain coveted insider information, blurring ethical lines and jeopardizing corporate integrity.

CHAPTER 4: THE INSIDER'S DOWNFALL

The name of Rajat Gupta, a highly esteemed businessman with board seats in Procter & Gamble, American Airlines, and Goldman Sachs, emerging in the scandal was a jaw-dropping moment. His impeccable reputation was overshadowed by his involvement in passing confidential information about Goldman Sachs' impending investment from Warren Buffett to Raj Rajaratnam. This act, done during the chaotic financial crisis of 2008, highlighted the pervasive lure of insider trading even among the seemingly unimpeachable.

The Buffett Effect

Gupta's insider tip about Warren Buffett's investment was a goldmine. Rajaratnam, acting on the tip, made lucrative trades before the public announcement. The reaction of the market to Buffett's investment was predictably positive, illustrating the immense potential for gains (or averting losses) that insider information could yield.

The Legal Reckoning

Rajat Gupta faced legal consequences for his actions, symbolizing a significant blow to the upper echelons of the business community. His conviction, alongside Rajaratnam's, sent ripples through Wall Street, emphasizing that no one was above the law when it came to insider trading.

The success in nabbing Rajaratnam and Gupta was a milestone, yet the FBI suggested it was merely the tip of the iceberg. The focus shifted towards "expert networks," revealing another layer in the complex structure of information exchange in the financial industry. The pervasive use of expert networks by traders exposed a systemic issue that went beyond individual malfeasances.

The reliance on expert networks by many in the trading profession unveiled a gray area in the quest for market intelligence. These networks, though legal, often tread a fine line, pushing the boundaries of what constituted fair information dissemination. Their widespread acceptance in the industry beckoned a closer examination of where the line should be drawn between legal consulting and the shady realm of insider trading.

The Gray Markets of Information

This unveils a fresh focus of the FBI investigation as it pivots towards the operation of "expert networks". These networks, known for connecting traders with insiders in various industries, operated in a legal yet largely unregulated domain. The commonality of their usage among traders showcased a gray area in financial dealings, blurring the line between legal consultancy and illegal insider trading.

Expert networks, around 40 operating nationwide, stood independent of traders and thrived on the lack of regulation. Their model involved acting as intermediaries, setting up dialogues between company insiders and big investors, such as hedge fund managers. Though rules existed outlining what could be shared, this underlines the persistent pressure and lure to cross these boundaries for more precise, actionable information.

With charges skyrocketing up to $5,000 for an hour-long consultation and some hedge fund clients shelling out up to a million dollars annually, the stakes in the expert network arena were high. This lucrative setup incentivized the delivery of information that could significantly impact stock movements, thus intensifying the allure of venturing into the realm of inside information.

It portrays expert networks as a double-edged sword. On one side, they fulfilled a legitimate need in the market by providing insights and analyses. Conversely, the same mechanism was exploited for insider trading, as illustrated by the FBI's use of cooperators who infiltrated these networks and recorded conversations.

The discussions between hedge fund managers and insiders, facilitated by expert networks, often tiptoed on the edge of legality. The desire for hard facts, rather than mere speculations, created a slippery slope leading to the procurement and utilization of inside information, thus posing a significant challenge for regulatory bodies.

Unveiling The Veil of Anonymity

As this progresses, the FBI embarks on a meticulous operation to unravel the workings of expert networks. Using covert tactics, they delve into the hidden dialogues between hedge fund managers and industry insiders, specifically targeting a prominent expert network, Primary Global Research (PGR).

In 2009, under a fabricated identity, an FBI informant approached PGR seeking their services. This operation was aimed at understanding the mechanics of how such networks operated and whether they facilitated the sharing of insider information. The informant's interaction with PGRs vice president, James Fleishman, served as a window into the ostensibly guarded yet porous system of expert networks.

Fleishman elucidates the modus operandi of PGR, emphasizing a system designed to maintain a veil of anonymity between the consultants and investors. However, the facade of this system begins to crack as Fleishman acknowledges the probability of information exchange going beyond the legal ambit, given the sheer volume of interactions.

The conversation unveils a precarious balance between the provision of useful insights and the breach of legal boundaries concerning proprietary information. While PGR had mechanisms purportedly to prevent the sharing of insider information, the hints at an underlying acknowledgment that the line could be, and likely was, crossed.

A significant revelation comes from an unpublished memoir of Fleishman, shared with Frontline, where he admits the likelihood of experts overstepping the bounds. Despite this acknowledgment, Fleishman asserts his innocence, setting a complex backdrop of legal and ethical dilemmas.

The FBI's Wiretap Operation

As the chapter draws to a close, it's revealed that the FBI had extended its surveillance to PGR's private conference lines, intensifying the scrutiny on the expert network. This move exemplifies the extensive measures taken to unearth the clandestine exchanges that could potentially be fueling insider trading.

Tangled Webs and Lobster Deals

Jiau, a contractor with deep-rooted connections in the technology realm, especially with firms having a foothold in Asia, becomes a pivotal figure. Her prior engagement with NVIDIA enabled her to maintain relationships that would later become conduits for insider information. Jiau's interactions primarily involved an SAC trader, Noah Freeman, who in turn shared the gleaned insights with his colleague Donald Longueuil.

An element of humor and peculiarity intertwines with the serious undertone of illicit dealings as Jiau demands compensation for her tips. Her requests, veiled under the metaphor of needing 'more sugar,' took a whimsical turn as she spurned a gift certificate for women's attire, opting instead for Cheesecake Factory gift certificates and live lobsters. This bizarre episode mirrors the bizarre lengths individuals were willing to traverse to keep the information flowing.

The accentuates the lucrative nature of the information Jiau provided, with Freeman acknowledging a windfall of five to ten million dollars over a four-year span from trading based on Jiau's tips. The exchange of insights for peculiar compensations unveils a surreal yet earnest quest for advantageous trading information.

The Long Arm of the Law Closes In

As the veil of secrecy begins to thin, the FBI makes its move in May 2010. The paints a vivid scene where, amid a mundane lunch break at a Subway sandwich shop, the clandestine operations of the characters begin to unravel as FBI agents make their presence known.

A Subway Encounter: Prelude to Reckoning

Amidst an ordinary day, a simple lunch break at a Subway shop unveils the stark reality to an involved trader. The appearance of FBI agents heralds the unraveling of the clandestine operations, bringing to the forefront the impending legal repercussions that loom over those entangled in the illicit network.

The unveils the hefty toll the law exacts upon the involved individuals. Fleishman and Jiau, central figures in the unfolding drama, find themselves facing the stark reality of federal prison. Yet, a contrasting fate awaits Freeman, whose cooperation with the law delays his sentencing.

The transitions to the pivotal moment when the Wall Street Journal breaks the silence, casting a glaring spotlight on the obscured dealings of Primary Global Research (PGR). The unfolding events send ripples across the finance sector, spurring a frantic scramble among those involved to erase evidence of their illicit endeavors.

The unfolding guides us deeper into the entangled networks, as the trail leads to the doorsteps of SAC Capital. Through the lens of informant Noah Freeman, a revealing glimpse into the inner workings of SAC is offered. The autonomy of "pods" within SAC, coupled with a lucrative incentive structure, unveils a conducive environment for illicit trading practices to thrive, albeit under a veil of plausible deniability for the higher echelons.

CHAPTER 5: A LABYRINTH UNVEILED

As the saga unfolds, the curtains draw back further, revealing more characters embroiled in the murky waters of insider trading. With every arrest and every trial, the far-reaching tendrils of illicit trading networks come into sharper focus. The now pivots to a close associate of Steven Cohen, Michael Steinberg, and subsequently to SAC portfolio manager Mathew Martoma, highlighting the relentless pursuit of justice by investigators.

The arrest of Michael Steinberg, a trusted confidante of Steven Cohen, marks a significant chapter in the . His position at SAC as a senior portfolio manager underscores the proximity of the investigation to Cohen. At the crux is an $11 million stake in Dell, believed to be sold based on illegal insider information. However, the defense puts forth a veil of plausible deniability, asserting the information was never seen by Cohen. Despite the contention, Steinberg faces the gavel, while Cohen remains unscathed, exemplifying the intricate nature of proving culpability in insider trading.

The tale transitions to Mathew Martoma, whose entanglement with expert networks digs deeper into the clandestine world of insider trading. Martoma's connection with Dr. Sidney Gilman through an expert network unveils a pathway to elicit information, outlining the quest for a lucrative Alzheimer's drug under development by Elan and Wyeth. This highlights the fragile line between seeking informational edges and crossing into the realm of illegal insider trading.

The unfolding accentuates the challenges and the meticulous efforts required to unveil and prosecute insider trading networks. The tales of Steinberg and Martoma are but threads in a broader tapestry of illicit trading practices that permeate the finance sector, reflecting a systemic issue that necessitates stringent regulatory scrutiny and ethical introspection.

Unseen Shadows

This now delves deeper into the realm of unseen knowledge and concealed interactions. The focus narrows down to the clandestine information exchange that allegedly took place between Martoma and Dr. Gilman, shedding light on the ripple effect it had on investors and the market at large.

Martoma's Conviction: The Hidden Exchange

Martoma's connection with Dr. Gilman through an expert network was more than just a professional liaison; it was a conduit for sensitive information that had the potential to shift market dynamics. Allegedly, Dr. Gilman divulged crucial results of the drug's second-round trial to Martoma before they were publicly released. This hidden exchange, if true, didn't just give Martoma a significant advantage but also painted a picture of how deeply ingrained such clandestine channels were in the trading ecosystem.

The Ripple Effect: Market Reactions

The secrecy surrounding the alleged information exchange between Martoma and Dr. Gilman underscored the massive risk that certain investors unknowingly bore. For instance, Greg Kappes, a pharmacist and private investor, had invested substantially in Elan, buoyed by the promising results of the initial drug trial and SAC's sizable investment. The revelation that crucial information might have been covertly passed to Martoma cast a dark shadow over the integrity of market operations and the unseen risks individual investors face.

SAC's Stance: A Veil of Assurance

Despite the reservations of several analysts and traders at SAC regarding the substantial unhedged positions in Elan and Wyeth, Cohen's unwavering faith in Martoma showcased the level of trust and the veil of assurance that Martoma's "insight" provided. The phrase "He's my guy" wasn't just an endorsement of Martoma's acumen but perhaps a reflection of the unspoken understanding of the clandestine channels of information that operated beneath the surface.

The episode sheds light on the dark corners of the financial industry where undisclosed information flows through hidden channels, bestowing undue advantage to a select few while leaving others in the dark. It is a stark reminder of the unseen forces that may drive market behavior and the vulnerabilities that exist within the system.

CHAPTER 6: TRADING IN SHADOWS

The ventures into the shadows of Wall Street, revealing a game where information is power and transparency is often a facade. As we explore the alleged actions of SAC Capital and its founder, Steven Cohen, a disturbing picture emerges of how the game was played behind the scenes.

Dr. Sidney Gilman, a figure of trust in the medical field, is accused of breaching that trust by allegedly sharing confidential information with Mathew Martoma. This information, hidden from the public eye, had the potential to make or break investments worth millions. The story illustrates how individuals with inside knowledge can tip the scales in their favor while leaving others in the dark.

The Mysterious Call: Cohen's Involvement

The pivotal moment arrives when Martoma allegedly shares the dire PowerPoint presentation from Dr. Gilman with Steven Cohen. This clandestine conversation is shrouded in secrecy, and the outcome is the rapid unwinding of SAC's positions in Elan and Wyeth. The question of what transpired during that conversation lingers, emphasizing the unchecked power held by those privy to hidden information.

Profits in the Shadows: SAC's Windfall

The government's claims are staggering: SAC Capital allegedly raked in an estimated $275 million based on inside information.

This underscores the vast sums of money at stake and how access to confidential data can enable enormous profits. It is a stark reminder of the unequal playing field in the financial world.

Greg Kappes, an individual investor, was among those who experienced the fallout. He had unwittingly entered a rigged game, and the consequences were financially devastating. Kappes' loss reflects the hidden risks that investors face when unaware of secret exchanges that impact their investments.

Cohen's Oblivion: Compliance Manual Ignored

The chapter concludes by shedding light on Steven Cohen's puzzling lack of awareness of SAC's compliance manual during a deposition. Cohen's apparent indifference to the rules and regulations governing his own firm raises questions about accountability and responsibility at the highest levels of the financial industry.

Compliance in Question

The deposition that followed a lawsuit filed by Fairfax Financial reveals the complexities and ambiguities surrounding SAC's trading practices.

Fairfax Financial had accused SAC Capital and other hedge funds of engaging in price manipulation through a "bear raid" on their stock. The chapter highlights the potentially unethical practice of short selling a stock based on advance knowledge of negative news. Steven Cohen's responses during the deposition come under scrutiny, shedding light on his approach to compliance.

Questioning Cohen: The Ambiguities Unveiled

Michael Bowe, representing Fairfax Financial, posed critical questions to Cohen about the acceptability of short selling with advance knowledge of negative news. Cohen's responses raise concerns about his understanding of compliance rules and his willingness to adhere to them. The chapter explores the implications of these responses.

The SEC, troubled by Cohen's deposition, filed a civil case against him, alleging a failure to supervise his traders. The government also took a significant step, filing a criminal indictment against SAC Capital, branding it a "magnet for market cheaters." The chapter delves into the legal actions against Cohen and SAC, marking a turning point in their legal battles.

The compliance issues faced by SAC Capital and Steven Cohen underscore the need for robust oversight and ethical conduct in financial markets. This prompts readers to consider the broader implications of lax compliance standards and their impact on market integrity.

The Prosecution's Stand

Dallas money manager Ed Butowsky emerges as a rare defender of SAC Capital, advocating for due process and emphasizing the importance of factual evidence. His public stance challenges the prevailing surrounding SAC's legal battles.

U.S. Attorney Preet Bharara asserts that SAC Capital engaged in insider trading on a substantial and pervasive scale without precedent. The chapter sheds light on the gravity of the charges against the hedge fund and its implications for the financial industry.

SAC Capital agrees to plead guilty as a corporation, marking the end of its tenure as a hedge fund. Additionally, Steven Cohen, as the sole owner, faces the largest insider trading fine in history—a staggering $1.8 billion.

U.S. Attorney Preet Bharara reaffirms the government's commitment to pursuing insider trading cases relentlessly. The ongoing investigations and the message that no one is above the law, regardless of their wealth or stature.

CONCLUSION

The Web of Greed and Accountability

In the concluding chapter of this gripping , the book weaves together the threads of greed, ambition, and accountability that have defined the world of finance. It's a world where fortunes are made and lost in the blink of an eye, where information is currency, and where the line between legality and criminality often blurs.

The book has taken us on a journey through the lives of traders, analysts, and hedge fund managers, revealing the intricate web of insider trading that has ensnared some of the industry's most prominent players. We've witnessed the rise and fall of individuals and firms, each entangled in a relentless pursuit of profit.

At the heart of this story is the question of accountability. We've seen how the legal system grapples with the challenge of holding individuals responsible for their actions within corporations. The cases of Raj Rajaratnam, Steven Cohen, and others illustrate the complexities of prosecuting white-collar crime and the ongoing debate over whether the punishments fit the crimes.

Moreover, the book has explored the role of regulators, prosecutors, and compliance officers in maintaining the integrity of financial markets. We've seen how their actions, or inaction, can shape the course of investigations and trials, and how their vigilance is essential in deterring misconduct.

Throughout the book , the book has posed thought-provoking questions about the nature of financial markets and the ethical choices made by those who operate within them. It challenges us to consider the fine line between seeking an edge in a competitive industry and engaging in illegal activity.

As we reach the end of this journey, the book leaves us with a sense of both fascination and concern. The world of finance is a realm where vast fortunes are built on information, where trust is fragile, and where the pursuit of profit can lead to moral and legal quagmires. It is a world that demands vigilance, transparency, and accountability, not only from its participants but also from the systems and institutions that govern it.

In closing, this book has provided a window into the complex and often murky world of finance, where the boundaries between right and wrong are not always clear-cut. It serves as a reminder that in the pursuit of wealth, integrity should never be sacrificed, and that accountability is essential to maintaining the trust and integrity of financial markets. It challenges us to consider how we, as a society, can ensure that the pursuit of profit does not come at the cost of ethical and legal principles.

Made in United States
Troutdale, OR
12/07/2024

26025121R00022